T0022924

ASTROLOGY
SELF-CARE

Aries

♈

ASTROLOGY
SELF-CARE

Aries

Live your best life
by the stars

Sarah Bartlett

First published in Great Britain in 2022 by Yellow Kite
An imprint of Hodder & Stoughton
An Hachette UK company

1

Illustrations © shutterstock.com

A CIP catalogue record for this title is
available from the British Library

Hardback ISBN 978 1 399 70458 8
eBook ISBN 978 1 399 70459 5
Audiobook ISBN 978 1 399 70460 1

Designed by Goldust Design

Typeset in Nocturne Serif by Hewer Text UK Ltd, Edinburgh
Printed and bound in Great Britain by Clays Ltd, Elcograf S.p.A.

Hodder & Stoughton policy is to use papers that are
natural, renewable and recyclable products and made
from wood grown in sustainable forests. The logging and
manufacturing processes are expected to conform to the
environmental regulations of the country of origin.

Yellow Kite
Hodder & Stoughton Ltd
. Carmelite House
50 Victoria Embankment
London EC4Y 0DZ

www.yellowkitebooks.co.uk

Let your hook be always cast. In the pool where you least expect it, there will be fish.

Ovid, Roman poet

There is a path, hidden between the road of reason and the hedgerow of dreams, which leads to the secret garden of self-knowledge. This book will show you the way.

Contents

Introduction

The ancient Greek goddess Gaia arose from Chaos and was the personification of the Earth and all of Nature. One of the first primordial beings, along with Tartarus (the Underworld), Eros (love) and Nyx (night), as mother of all life, she is both the embodiment of all that this planet is and its spiritual caretaker.

It's hardly likely you will want to become a full-time Mother Earth, but many of us right now are caring more about our beautiful planet and all that lives upon it. To nurture and respect this amazing place we call home, and to preserve this tiny dot in the Universe, the best place to start is, well, with you.

Self-care is about respecting and honouring who you are as an individual. It's about realising that nurturing yourself is neither vanity nor a conceit, but a creative act that brings an awesome sense of awareness and a deeper connection to the Universe and all that's in it. Caring about yourself means you care about everything in the cosmos – because you are part of it.

But self-care isn't just about trekking to the gym, jogging around the park or eating the right foods. It's also about discovering who you are becoming as an individual and caring for that authenticity (and loving and caring about who we are becoming means others can love and care about us, too). This is where the art of sun-sign astrology comes in.

Astrology and Self-Care

So what is astrology? And how can it direct each of us to the right self-care pathway? Put simply, astrology is the study of the planets, sun and moon and their influence on events and people here on Earth. It is an art that has been used for thousands of years to forecast world events, military and political outcomes and, more recently, financial market trends. As such, it is an invaluable tool for understanding our own individuality and how to be true to ourselves. Although there is still dispute within astrological circles as to whether the planets actually physically affect us, there is strong evidence to show that the cycles and patterns they create in the sky have a direct mirroring effect on what happens down here on Earth and, more importantly, on each individual's personality.

Your horoscope or birth-chart is a snapshot of the planets, sun and moon in the sky at the moment you were born. This amazing picture reveals all your innate potential, characteristics and qualities. In fact, it is probably the best 'selfie' you could ever have! Astrology can not only tell you who you are, but also how best to care for that self and your own specific needs and desires as revealed by your birth-chart.

Self-care is simply time to look after yourself – to restore, inspirit and refresh and love your unique self. But it's also about understanding, accepting and

11

being aware of your own traits – both the good and not so good – so that you can then say, 'It's ok to be me, and my intention is to become the best of myself'. In fact, by looking up to the stars and seeing how they reflect us down here on Earth, we can deepen our connection to the Universe for the good of all, too. Understanding that caring about ourselves is not selfish creates an awesome sense of self-acceptance and awareness.

So how does each of us honour the individual 'me' and find the right kind of rituals and practices to suit our personalities? Astrology sorts us out into the zodiac – an imaginary belt encircling the Earth divided into twelve sun signs; so, for example, what one sign finds relaxing, another may find a hassle or stressful. When it comes to physical fitness, adventurous Arians thrive on aerobic work, while soulful Pisceans feel nurtured by yoga. Financial reward or status would inspire the ambitious Capricorn mind, while theatrical Leos need to indulge their joy of being centre stage.

By knowing which sun sign you are and its associated characteristics, you will discover the right self-care routines and practices to suit you. And this unique and empowering book is here to help – with all the rituals and practices in these pages specifically suited to your sun-sign personality for nurturing and vitalising your mind, body and spirit.

However, self-care is not an excuse to be lazy and avoid the goings on in the rest of the world. Self-care is about taking responsibility for our choices and understanding our unique essence, so that we can engage with all aspects of ourselves and the way we interact with the world.

IN A NUTSHELL

The Aries fast-and-furious race to get anywhere first means physical challenge and pioneering ideas boost your dynamic energy and, in turn, provide you with the self-nurturing you thrive on. Here, you will find exciting ways to inspire you with new goals, understand your relationship with the world and excel at all you wish to do. There are no set routines in this book, only a wide range of ideas and practices to set you off on a trailblazing adventure to discover who you are truly becoming. Being aware of who you are, means you are truly caring for that self, too.

Sun-Sign Astrology

Also known as your star sign or zodiac sign, your sun sign encompasses the following:

* Your solar identity, or sense of self
* What really matters to you
* Your future intentions
* Your sense of purpose
* Various qualities that manifest through your actions, goals, desires and the personal sense of being 'you'
* Your sense of being 'centred' – whether 'self-centred' (too much ego) or 'self-conscious' (too little ego); in other words, how you perceive who you are as an individual

In fact, the sun tells you how you can 'shine' best to become who you really are.

ASTROLOGY FACTS

The zodiac or sun signs are twelve 30-degree segments that create an imaginary belt around the Earth. The zodiac belt is also known as the ecliptic, which is the apparent path of the sun as it travels round the Earth during the year.

The sun or zodiac signs are further divided into four elements (Fire, Earth, Air and Water, denoting a certain energy ruling each sign), plus three modalities (qualities associated with how we inter-act with the world; these are known as Cardinal, Fixed and Mutable). So as an Arian, for example, you are a 'Cardinal Fire' sign.

* Fire signs: Aries, Leo, Sagittarius
  They are: extrovert, passionate, assertive

* Earth signs: Taurus, Virgo, Capricorn
  They are: practical, materialistic, sensual

* Air signs: Gemini, Libra, Aquarius
  They are: communicative, innovative, inquisitive

* Water signs: Cancer, Scorpio, Pisces
  They are: emotional, intuitive, understanding

The modalities are based on their seasonal resonance according to the northern hemisphere.

Cardinal signs instigate and initiate ideas and projects.
They are: Aries, Cancer, Libra and Capricorn

Fixed signs resolutely build and shape ideas.
They are: Taurus, Leo, Scorpio and Aquarius

Mutable signs generate creative change and adapt ideas to reach a conclusion.

They are: Gemini, Virgo, Sagittarius and Pisces

Planetary rulers

Each zodiac sign is assigned a planet, which highlights the qualities of that sign:

Aries is ruled by Mars (fearless)
Taurus is ruled by Venus (indulgent)
Gemini is ruled by Mercury (magical)
Cancer is ruled by the moon (instinctive)
Leo is ruled by the sun (empowering)
Virgo is ruled by Mercury (informative)
Libra is ruled by Venus (compassionate)
Scorpio is ruled by Pluto (passionate)
Sagittarius is ruled by Jupiter (adventurous)
Capricorn is ruled by Saturn (disciplined)
Aquarius is ruled by Uranus (innovative)
Pisces is ruled by Neptune (imaginative)

Opposite Signs

Signs oppose one another across the zodiac (i.e. those that are 180 degrees away from each other) – for example, Aries opposes Libra and Taurus opposes Scorpio. We often find ourselves mysteriously attracted to our opposite signs in romantic relationships, and while the signs' traits appear to clash in this 'polarity', the essence of each is contained in the other (note, they have the same modality). Gaining insight into the characteristics of your opposite sign (which are, essentially, inherent in you) can deepen your understanding of the energetic interplay of the horoscope.

On The Cusp

Some of us are born 'on the cusp' of two signs – in other words, the day or time when the sun moved from one zodiac sign to another. If you were born at the end or beginning of the dates usually given in horoscope pages (the sun's move through one sign usually lasts approximately four weeks), you can check which sign you are by contacting a reputable astrologer (or astrology site) (see Resources, p. 117) who will calculate it exactly for you. For example, 23 August is the standardised changeover day for the sun to move into Virgo and out of Leo. But every year, the time and even sometimes the day the sun changes sign can differ. So, say you were born on 23 August at five in the morning and the sun didn't move into Virgo until five in the afternoon on that day, you would be a Leo, not a Virgo.

How To Use This Book

The book is divided into three parts, each guiding you in applying self-care to different areas of your life:

* Part One: your mind and feelings
* Part Two: your body
* Part Three: your soul

Caring about the mind using rituals or ideas tailored to your sign shows you ways to unlock stress, restore focus or widen your perception. Applying the practices in Part One will connect you to your feelings and help you to acknowledge and become aware of why your emotions are as they are and how to deal with them. This sort of emotional self-care will set you up to deal with your relationships better, enhance all forms of communication and ensure you know exactly how to ask for what you want or need, and be true to your deepest desires.

A WORD ON CHAKRAS

Eastern spiritual traditions maintain that universal energy, known as 'prana' in India and 'chi' in Chinese philosophy, flows through the body, linked by seven subtle energy centres known as chakras (Sanskrit for 'wheel'). These energies are believed to revolve or spiral around and through our bodies, vibrating at different frequencies (corresponding to seven colours of the light spectrum) in an upward, vertical direction. Specific crystals are placed on the chakras to heal, harmonise, stimulate or subdue the chakras if imbalance is found.

The seven chakras are:

* The base or root (found at the base of the spine)
* The sacral (mid-belly)
* The solar plexus (between belly and chest)
* The heart (centre of chest)
* The throat (throat)
* The third eye (between the eyebrows)
* The crown (top of the head)

On p. 87 we will look in more detail at how Arians can work with chakras for self-care.

Fitness and caring for the body are different for all of us, too. While Aries benefits from competitive sport, for example, Taurus thrives on aromatherapy sessions and Gemini a daily quick stretch or yoga. Delve into Part Two whenever you're in need of physical restoration or a sensual makeover tailored to your sign.

Spiritual self-care opens you to your sacred self or soul. Which is why Part Three looks at how you can nurture your soul according to your astrological sun sign. It shows you how to connect to and care for your spirituality in simple ways, such as being at one with Nature or just enjoying the world around you. It will show you how to be more positive about who you are and honour your connection to the Universe. In fact, all the rituals and practices in this section will bring you joyful relating, harmonious living and a true sense of happiness.

The Key

Remember, your birth-chart or horoscope is like the key to a treasure chest containing the most precious jewels that make you you. Learn about them, and care for them well. Use this book to polish, nurture, respect and give value to the beautiful gemstones of who you are, and, in doing so, bring your potential to life. It's your right to be true to who you are, just by virtue of being born on this planet, and therefore being a child of Mother Earth and the cosmos.

Care for you, and you care for the Universe.

ARIES
WORDS OF WISDOM

As you embark on your self-care journey, it's important to look at the lunar cycles and specific astrological moments throughout the year. At those
times (and, indeed, at any time you choose), the
words of Aries wisdom below will be invaluable,
empowering you with positive energy. Taking a few
mindful moments at each of the four major phases
of every lunar cycle and at the two important astrological moments in your solar year (see Glossary,
p. 119) will affirm and enhance your positive attitude towards caring about yourself and the world.

NEW CRESCENT MOON – to care for yourself:

'I have the courage to champion patience and be tolerant of others.'

'Life is for doing things, not merely dreaming about doing them.'

'If I look before I leap, I will always succeed in my goal.'

FULL MOON – for sealing your intention to care for your feeling world:

'My feelings of love or desire can be expressed if I trust my intuition.'

'My inner resources are abundant; I have everything I need for a fulfilling life.'

'The compassion I have for others reflects the compassion I have for myself.'

WANING MOON – for letting go, and letting things be:

'I release my grudges and relinquish my intolerance of those whose desires may be different to mine.'

'I will not speak out, unless I can improve on the silence.'

'I will remember to be grateful for others who may show me the way.'

DARK OF THE MOON AFFIRMATION – to acknowledge your 'shadow' side:

'I will try not to make a drama or crusade over trivial issues, nor blow them up to be major problems.'

'The energy of the Universe flows through me, sustaining my wellbeing, as I leave a trail of healing energy for all.'

'From the infinite depths of my sacred self I send powerful, loving energies to all the friends around me.'

SOLAR RETURN SALUTATION – each year when the sun moves through your sign, it's time to salute or welcome in your next solar year and to be true to who you are:

Repeat on your birthday: 'My will is strong, my self-belief unfailing and I choose to follow my dreams. This year I will achieve all the things I really believe are right for me.'

SUN IN OPPOSITION – learn to be open to the opposite perspective that lies within you:

'My opposite sign is Libra, a sign of equality and tolerance. These things are part of my birth-chart, too, so I must learn to compromise and be fairer about others' viewpoints. I also resolve to let others speak their minds and not talk over them.'

The Aries Personality

Υ

Always forgive your enemies;
nothing annoys them so much.
Oscar Wilde, Irish poet and playwright

Characteristics: Feisty, assertive, motivated, courageous, extrovert, egocentric, proud, impulsive, competitive, blunt, dynamic, insensitive, impatient, challenging, easily angered, pioneering, energetic, carefree, wilful, goal-oriented

Symbol: the Ram

In Greek mythology, Aries is identified with the Golden Fleece, the ram sacrificed to the gods in the epic tale of Jason and the Argonauts. Zeus honoured the Ram by placing him in the heavens as the constellation Aries.

Planetary ruler: Mars

Named after the Roman god of war, this red planet may look hot, but it is, in fact, very cold. Mars has two small moons, Phobos and Deimos, which apparently resemble potatoes rather than spheres, due to a lack of gravitational mass. The moons get their names from the two charioteers who took the Greek god of war, Ares, into battle.

Astrological Mars: In the birth-chart, Mars describes where and how we go about getting what we want, not forgetting how we 'go into battle'. It tells us where we might meet resistance or an easy passage, and the way we fight for our beliefs or desires.

Element: Fire
Like the other Fire signs, Leo and Sagittarius, Aries has inexhaustible enthusiasm, and just wants to get on with life, rather than stop and think about it. Fire people are spontaneous and have active imaginations, always looking to the future and rarely to the past.

Modality: Cardinal
Marking the beginning of the astrological year and the spring equinox (in the northern hemisphere), Aries is a self-starter, with a sense of purpose and the urge to lead others.

Body: In astrology, each sign rules various parts of the body. Aries traditionally rules the head, brain and muscular system.

Crystal: Red carnelian

Sun-sign profile: Feisty Aries is not only goal-oriented, assertive and impulsive, but this outgoing, impatient sign has to be first in everything they do – first in the queue, first to arrive at the party, first to know everything about everyone they meet. A social animal, the Ram loves being surrounded by an entourage of adoring pals, but their blunt way of asking personal questions can create animosity. The Arian 'ignore-me-at-your-peril' attitude resonates with their status as the first sign of the zodiac. It's hardly surprising, then, that this action-packed sign, ruled by the god of war, is renowned for being a little arrogant, egotistic and insensitive.

An incredible pioneer, who bravely goes where no one has gone before, you'll climb every mountain to reach a goal, impulsively pursue your ideals and avoid living an ordinary existence. Other people may see you as larger than life, courageous and spirited, and it's that devil-may-care attitude that gets you places and infuriates your rivals.

Your best-kept secret: Aries is really no more 'self-centred' than anyone else. We all have egos, or we wouldn't be able to get on in life. However, as an

Arian you know and utterly believe you have a very specific purpose in life, and that's yourself. This secret weapon is like a missile – once released, it hits its target and nothing and no one is going to stop you. And anyone who tries will have to bear the brunt of your 'all-or-nothing' tactics.

What gives you meaning and purpose in life?
Yourself most of all. A goal, a challenge, looking to the future, living out your dream. Leading the crowd. Being first to be on trend. Your solar purpose is to shine your 'solo' light wherever you go, so that you make an impact and live out your vision of being a heroic figure, saving the world from broken dreams.

What makes you feel good to be you? Being physically fit, trailblazing, laughter and social fun; not having responsibilities or duties, being carefree. Winning, arguing (as long as you win), competition and being passionate about love and life. Rivalry – proving you're the best.

What or who do you identify with? Warriors, heroes, heroines, fighters, sports celebrities, great explorers, lawyers, military leaders, battles, firm muscles, fast cars, motorbikes, Boadicea

What stresses you out? Failure – your own and other people's. Not getting your way. Waiting. The 'real' world and all its problems; not being in control.

What relaxes you? Physical exercise, your fantasy world, imagination, a new goal or project, being on top of a mountain, making a must-do list (and crossing everything off when the mission is completed), watching your rivals lose

What challenges you? Evasiveness, secrets, flaws, human emotions generally, people who don't agree with you; the physical world, wimps, losing, being last, giving in, not getting to where you want to be

What Does Self-Care Mean For Aries?

With a 'let's-get-on-with-it' attitude to life, Arians rarely have time to sit around thinking about an orderly self-care programme, let alone follow long instructions for meditation or home harmony. The Ram is more likely to be found trying out highly active or extreme sports such as bungee jumping, surfing, skydiving or rock climbing in their pursuit of excitement and challenge.

Although not an intentional self-care devotee, as an Arian you practise physical self-care by default through an active lifestyle, which does wonders for your seemingly inexhaustible enthusiasm and energy. Burning up calories faster than most other zodiac signs, you don't have much of a problem with weight, but you need to be more conscious of what you eat and when to fuel those flames of potent energy.

Self-Care Focus

If self-care sounds like it's for wimps, then think again. If you want a brand-new quest, maybe it's time to find out who you really are and what you can do with that potential to make your life journey as exciting as you want it to be? With this in mind, let's boldly replace the words 'self-care' with 'self-discovery'.

Looking after your mind and spirit, as well as your body, could be the challenge you currently need to get you moving through life at the speed you like. It's not about *changing* who you are, but about *being* who you are, and embracing the qualities that make you you.

The self-care practices in this book will inspire you to trailblaze, light your flame, be influential and show off your personal magnetism, not forgetting being a catalyst for change. If you get a buzz from physical self-expression, then that's caring for your body; if you get high on leading the pack, then you care about how you feel when relating to others. And if you experience a moment of being at one with the Universe, then that's acknowledging and caring for your spirit and soul.

So stoke the fire within and be true to your solar self. The practices in this book will inspire and give blessing to your unique life journey, preparing you to accomplish any mission, however impossible it may seem.

PART ONE

Caring For Your Mind And Feelings

'The adventures first,' said the Gryphon in an impatient tone: 'explanations take such a dreadful time.'

Lewis Carroll, *Alice's Adventures in Wonderland*

This section will inspire you to delight in your thoughts, express your ideas and take pleasure in your feelings. Once you get that deep sense of awareness of who you are and what you need, not only will it feel good to be alive, but you will be even more content to be yourself. The rituals and practices here will boost your self-esteem, motivate you to lead a more serene existence and enhance all forms of relationships with others. The most important relationship of all, with yourself, will be nurtured in the best possible way according to your sun sign.

Like fellow Fire sign Sagittarius, Aries often lives an almost mythical lifestyle, always searching for a goal, a new adventure, a new thrill. The more dangerous or challenging the goal, the more motivated and animated their spirit becomes. Epic heroes and heroines, such as Jason and the Argonauts in search of the Golden Fleece (related to your symbol, the Ram) or the incomparable Scarlett O'Hara in *Gone With the Wind* are superb archetypes of the Aries spirit.

Frankly, as you need to get straight to the point, we're going to focus on channelling your fiery gifts, enhancing your quest for a new goal, restoring that inimitable spirit when you need it and polishing your Aries mind, ready for battle with the dragons of life.

....

VISION-QUEST MOOD BOARD

In many indigenous cultures, initiates would be sent out into the wilderness on a 'vision quest' to discover their true selves in readiness for their calling. To avoid a long, boring sit in the middle of nowhere, you could try creating a vision-quest mood board instead.

Pin up images, notes, words – anything that represents your current goal – on a board or large sheet of paper. Alternatively, you could use magnets to stick photos and papers on your fridge.

If you don't have a current 'quest', then find time to visualise one. Think about all the possible adventures you would like to have, or the many challenges in the world that might excite you. If any desire takes precedence, or a particular issue gets your adrenalin racing, create a mood board to reflect that.

The more often you see this visual display of your goal – adding new information or taking away ideas as it changes – the better. You will discover more about your own wanderlust nature and see it as a unique expression of yourself at every step along your chosen pathway.

YOUR VERY OWN MYTH

The epic myth of Jason and the Argonauts resonates with the Aries search for action and adventure. Briefly, the search for the elusive Golden Fleece (the skin of the mystical golden ram that eventually became the constellation Aries) was a seemingly impossible quest for the hero, Jason. On the journey, with the help of the enchantress Medea, he fought tricksters, monsters and evil beasts, while experiencing betrayal by others, and also betraying Medea himself. As with any hero's journey, Jason found out who he was. He embodied the spirit of adventure, but he was only human, too.

Here's a quick candle ritual to connect to the fire within. Do this whenever you feel the urge to get up and go.

You will need:

* 3 golden threads (to represent the Golden Fleece)
* 3 red tea lights
* 3 red carnelians

1. Using the three threads, make a triangle shape, with one point facing north.

2. Place the three candles in the centre of the triangle and a red carnelian stone at each point on the triangle.

3. Light the candles.

4. Now relax, gaze into the flames and say: 'My quest is never-ending, my passion and self-belief are boundless and my fire within will bring understanding about my true heroic journey'.

5. Contemplate the words you've just said for a minute or so, then blow out the candles to seal your intention – not only to yourself, but to the Universe, too.

A heroic journey is a vivid metaphor for the Aries solar purpose. Use this mythical quality to set your world alight.

SEEING RED

Due to the rusting iron deposits in the cold, dry rocks and soil of planet Mars, the dust swirls up into the atmosphere and makes the planet appear red. Illusion or not, the hot-headed energy of Mars and your Fire sign is reflected in the colour red. Red is also associated with fire, passion, excitement, thrills, bright lights, racing ahead and power. Yet a red traffic light tells us to stop at a dangerous crossing or junction.

Aries rarely stops for anything, and of course, your inexorable faith and self-belief are channelled into the joy of being you. But sometimes you have to come to a halt at the red light, so you can experience the joy of moving on again. Here's a quick and easy visualisation to help with this before you leap off to embrace your next amazing plan, goal or challenge. It won't put you off your mission, but it will give you the chance to reflect before acting.

1. Sit or just stand still for a moment. Close your eyes.

2. Imagine you're driving a very fast car – so fast you could even win the Grand Prix.

3. You are at the front, leading the others. You are about to win when a marshal waves a red flag. There is danger ahead, and you know you have to slow down. It frustrates you, but you have a conscience and don't want to cause any more danger than there is already.

4. You slow down, and as you do so, you say to yourself, 'Yes, I've had to slow down to be careful. I can move on again when the danger has passed. Now is the time for a pit stop – a time to reflect on the next step ahead.'

Do this visualisation before you set off on a new venture. With a little more forethought, you will get to where you want to be with positive ramifications, rather than arriving too soon with regretful afterthoughts.

THE THUNDER STONE

Arians are generally thought to have luck on their side. But sometimes it's worth boosting that innate quality with a little help from the cosmos.

There is an ancient folklore belief that if you find a specific smooth or hollowed stone at the place where lightning has struck, it will bestow on you good fortune and protection. Carrying or wearing this stone will bring you more luck than you could imagine.

Try the following practice to manifest this talisman for yourself.

You will need:
* A piece of paper
* A pen/pencil/paints

1. Draw or paint an image of thunder and a bolt of lightning on your piece of paper. It doesn't have to be a masterpiece; a sketch or some vibrant lines will do – a conscious awareness of putting pen to paper.

2. At the point where the lightning bolt meets the Earth, draw a stone – any shape you like.

3. Touch the image of the stone, as if you are discovering it, and imagine holding it close to you.

4. Fold up your paper and keep it in a safe place.

Wherever you go, imagine this thunder stone as a pendant around your neck to bring you fortune and opportunity.

CARE FOR YOUR CHARISMA

You're renowned for the charismatic effect you have on the world around you, which, in turn, makes you feel good to be you.

Caring for your innate charisma is the first step to getting on with life in the here and now. But you need to make sure you don't exaggerate your sense of self-importance (too much ego can overshadow a true awareness of what your goals are), while maintaining your glamorous appeal. Knot spells bind and focus our intentions, but they also seal our precious gifts and qualities with the riches of the Universe to receive goodness back. Try this simple ritual:

You will need:
* A 90cm (36 inch) length of gold cord, wool, twine or string

1. Make nine knots (nine is the number of adventure and journeys) – any old kind will do – along the length of the cord, as evenly spaced as possible.

2. Taking hold of each knot in turn, repeat: 'I enjoy life fully and with gratitude to the Universe, for my charisma is mine to share with the world'.

3. Finally, hold each knot and say, 'I share my charisma'.

4. This ritual will enhance your allure and simultaneously give you the chance to manifest your goals.

GOOD INTENTIONS FOR ALL

Whatever our sun sign, our opposite sign gives us a clue as to what we might need to learn to value more in ourselves. In fact, we often project these apparently disparate qualities on to the outside world or on to other people, and refuse to accept they are part of our own psyches.

In your case, Aries pleases itself, while its opposite sign, Libra, pleases others (albeit with the ulterior motive of pleasing itself). So if you were to step into Libra's shoes for a second, you might realise that the good intentions you have for yourself could actually be shared a little with others. Wouldn't 'spreading the word' give you more possibilities and opportunities to explore as people give you feedback and open doors for you?

So whenever you're on a mission, say, as often as you can: 'I have good intentions for myself and for everyone else'.

It will make any mission far more possible.

. . . .

THE BIG 'I' TEST

Hubris is an exaggerated sense of pride, as demonstrated by the mortal Icarus, who didn't heed his father's warning about the danger of flying too close to the sun and, with his disdainful 'I will do it my way', burned his wings and fell to Earth. Likewise, Arians sometimes fly too high, and, when they expect too much of others or of themselves, can plummet to Earth and risk losing those glorious wings. Here's how to fly close enough to the metaphorical sun without getting burned.

You will need:
* A large piece of paper
* A pen

1. In the middle of the paper draw a huge 'I' to represent you and mark a circle around it to represent the sun.

2. Write at the top of the page: 'This is me now'.

3. Over the course of the day, or whenever you have time, write little 'i's around the outside of the circle, and alongside each 'i' a verb or action to sum up that moment. So you might write, 'i think', 'i desire' or 'i am hungry' – anything that comes to mind.

4. Once you have filled the page with little 'i's, see how the big 'I' doesn't seem quite so important now. The little ones have meaning – they act, they move you along and they don't let you burn up in the heat of the moment. It is these 'i's that 'do' the actions.

Be kind to your little 'i'. It is there to guard and guide you. It is the authentic 'i' that says, 'the Universe brings me the life that I choose'. It is the arrogant 'I' that can lead you to burn your wings.

THE MOONS OF MARS

The two 'potato-shaped' moons of Mars are named after the sons of the Greek war god, Ares. Phobos was the personification of fear, while Deimos was the embodiment of dread. These two instincts lie at the core of the Aries reckless, adrenalin-rush-seeking, impulsive nature.

Sometimes the pushy Phobos and Deimos want to drive your chariot too fast. So to achieve greater things, rather than rush into battle without a thought for what might happen, you need to regain control of your chariot of fire. Here's how:

Just as you're getting riled up about something – the state of the nation, for example – force yourself to stop what you're doing. Step back and take a few deep, slow breaths. Imagine you, and not those two potato-head adrenalin junkies, are now in control of your chariot. Talk to them firmly; remind them they are only moons, while you are the planet Mars, in all your glory. By the time you've admonished your moons, you will be in a position to reflect your true battle strategy.

IDENTITY PARADE

As you don't believe in an ordinary life, you may be one of those Arians who create all kinds of identities around yourself. One day you might say, 'Well, next week I'm going to be a bit of a warrior for a cause', while another day you might say, 'I feel like a hero' and so on. The problem arises when too many labels or identities get in the way of you knowing who you really are.

Self-discovery comes from releasing yourself from labels and false IDs and focusing on what really matters to you – and isn't that to discover the true Aries within?

So maybe find a moment each day to write on a scrap of paper a character or label you may have used for yourself, and then crumple it up and throw it in the bin. Free yourself from these identities and see how you free up your spirit of adventure, unhampered by roles and labels. Now you can be just who you are.

THE FORTRESS

Fire signs are convinced that they are invincible, and hardly have time to worry about defences and boundaries. So before you embark on yet another Don-Quixote-like adventure, try the following ritual to build a symbolic fortress around yourself for protection and strength.

You will need:

* A small personal keepsake or something of sentimental value (for example, a ring, a book, a photo, a coin, a pen . . .)
* A red tea light
* A 60cm (24 inch) length of gold ribbon, cord, twine or thread
* A box, pouch or container

1. Place your chosen keepsake on a table.

2. Light the candle and say, 'I light the candle to see the way'.

3. Wind the ribbon around and around the keepsake until you've circled it at least three times, and say:

> I wind this gold to seal my fortress,
> To defend and give me boundaries
> To safely find the pathway forward.

4. Slowly unwind the ribbon, take up your keepsake and ribbon and place them in the container, now a symbol of the empowering fortress that surrounds you.

You are ready for your next great adventure, knowing your stronghold will protect and strengthen your resources.

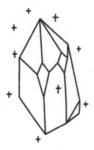

POSITIVE INTERACTIONS

Make sure you make it a regular mission to have a good debate with friends or colleagues to revive and stimulate your Aries mind. The odd argument or challenging new ideas will release those 'feelgood-factor' hormones and enliven your fiery spirit. However, remember that other people have their own ideas, dreams and hopes, too. Don't dampen theirs; accept their viewpoint graciously, but make it clear to others – and to yourself – that you have established your own.

To enhance positive interaction and great thoughts, whenever you're socialising or debating take with you a piece of green aventurine; this represents both opportunity and compassion.

AFFIRMATIONS

Aries makes a very good teacher of ideas, visions and projects. Use this skill on yourself, teaching yourself affirmations to invoke a vitalised attitude. Here are some to get you started:

* 'I will learn to develop cooperation and respect for others' needs.'
* 'I need to accept that sometimes detours and diversions are other ways to reach a goal, apart from steaming straight ahead.'
* 'I am not missing out on something if I'm not the first to arrive.'
* 'I will balance activity with passivity, assertiveness with gentleness.'
* 'Everything that is meant to happen will happen, when it is meant to happen.'
* 'Frustration only stems from resisting what is.'

YOUR FUTURE ORACLE

There are many divination techniques, such as palm-reading, casting runes and reading tarot cards, aimed at discovering the secrets of one's past, present and future. Divination is a way to tap into the energy of the moment via symbolic messages to discover what the Universe is saying to you. As the Ram's focus is looking to the future, light your way forward with an easy divination technique known as bibliomancy, involving simply opening a book at a random page.

You will need:
* A fairly chunky text-only book – perhaps a dictionary, epic novel or encyclopaedia
* A pen
* A piece of paper

Write down the following questions on the piece of paper, leaving room for answers after each one:
    * What challenges are in store for me?
    * What areas of my life would benefit from thinking bigger than I already do?
    * How can I be more open to others' points of view?

* What is the best way to live my passion and fight for what I believe?
* How can I best free up my fear of being only human?
* How do I learn from my mistakes?

2. Ask the first question, then randomly open the book.

3. With eyes closed, run your finger around the page and stop when you intuitively feel it is the right moment.

4. Read the words or sentence that's closest to your finger and relate it to your question.

5. As you ask the questions (you can concentrate on just one a day, or go through all of them at once), write down the words or sentences the book reveals to you for each one, and review your oracle when the session is finished. You'll be surprised at how it resonates and gives you a symbolic meaning each time.

You will now be in a beneficial position to make plans for the next step of your future pathway, knowing the Universe has provided you with the truth.

RITUAL FOR SUCCESS

As an Arian, you're always in one big hurry to achieve something. Hard-working and energetic, you're willing to take risks others wouldn't dream of, and are brilliant at inventing new ways of doing traditional things, whether in politics, sport or business. So if you're a success-driven Aries, why not make ambition the key element of your life?

If you have a desire or goal you truly, truly want to realise, then create an image of it in your mind. Include all the props – whether they're material possessions or experiences.

For example, you might want to be a successful business tycoon: picture the outfit you'd be wearing, a few boardroom and even bedroom scenarios, an amount of money in the bank. Imagine achieving all this alone. Or, if your goal is to be a mountaineer, imagine specific mountains, the equipment you'd use, the scenery you would be inspired by.

Perhaps your goal is more to do with relationships. If it's romance you're after, imagine the person of your dreams – what do they look like? What's their hair colour? Their eye colour? What do they say to you? What do you say to them? Create your own script. Or, if it's to improve an existing relationship, imagine you and the other person in a beautiful setting: you both have the same objectives or ideas; you each feel mutual acceptance, forgiveness or respect for the other.

Practise holding the vision or thought in your mind of what you desire. Devote as much time as you can each day to visualising and concentrating on such images and thoughts. The more you practise visualising success, the sooner you will achieve it.

ANGER RELEASE

There are probably many times when you lose your temper, exploding over trifles, when tiny issues become overwhelming mountains of 'everyone else is to blame', and the build-up of tension has nowhere to go, it seems. So you scream at someone, or throw your toys out of the pram. The simple technique below will deflect anger, or any kind of negative feeling, without smashing plates.

Keep a 'special' stone (perhaps a pebble or a 'palm stone' (a flat crystal shaped specifically to sit in the palm of your hand, available at new-age stores – see Resources, p. 117) in your pocket or bag at all times. Whenever you feel those rogue emotions building up inside you, take the stone in your hand and squeeze it tightly – as hard as you can – and only release it once you feel the emotion or anger moving away from you. Once you have stopped squeezing the stone, turn it over and over in the palm of your hand for a minute or so, as if making friends with it. All ranting-and-raving feelings will change to peaceful ones.

Relationships

In romantic love, Arians revel in the chase; the more elusive or 'hard to get' the object of their desire is, the more they are up for the hunt, rather than the actual conquest. The Ram seeks the ideals of romance, the fantasies of courtly love and knights in shining armour. Sadly, as this doesn't actually exist, they become disillusioned by the reality of commitment and long-term love or they abandon their mission and set off on another love quest. But if an Arian meets someone who respects their need for loads of space, and is as independent and motivated as they are, the Ram will be loyalty personified. Aries is in with a chance of long-term partnership when two 'me firsts' can each get on with their lives in their own unique way.

....

AROUSE DESIRE

To stir desire in someone else's heart, carry this magic enchantment with you on a first date.

'The Green Man' is a symbolic foliate head often found in Christian iconography. However, it probably originates from pre-Christian Nature gods such as the Celtic horned god, Cernunnos, and the earlier Greek god Pan. Pagan horned gods were associated with rebirth and the coming of spring, as well as wild passion, sexuality and fertility. This fascinating head will endow you with the ability to bewitch and draw anyone to you. There are times when a little help from the wanton god of desire will encourage more of the chase and less of the capture.

Try the following to either enjoy hunting out new romance or to endow a love relationship with physical bliss.

You will need:
* 2 sage or bay leaves
* A tiny 'Green Man' image
* 2 small, rough rubies or sunstones
* A silk or muslin pouch

1. Crush the leaves or crumple them up.

2. Place the crushed leaves, along with your 'Green Man' and two stones, in the pouch.

3. Keep the pouch hidden, either in your bag or on your person, throughout the time you are on a date and let the magic begin.

Not only will your Aries charm work wonders, but this earthy divine energy will instil in you a glamorous allure. Oh – and if you want to boost your physical love life, leave the pouch hidden beside your bed.

....

CULTIVATE EMPATHY
AND FORGIVENESS

Now Arians have a hard time imagining themselves in someone else's shoes, and really don't have time to worry about other people's feelings when their own are hard enough to deal with. When it comes to caring about the darker recesses of the mind, then, that's for other people to concern themselves with, and the less said about their own, the better. After all, emotions – those troublesome gatecrashers – can get in the way of having a good time at their party of one.

However, a little compassion, patience and tolerance of others, and accepting differences of opinion, means cultivating empathy for yourself, too. We can say that you have a conveniently foggy view of the vulnerable side of human nature and of course, that's part of who you are. But if you were to try a little more forgiveness, not blame people for 'stuff' and be a little more sensitive to the rhythms and voices of others, you might find that a few more doors begin to open for you, rather than you trying to bash them down.

Use this simple visualisation to help you switch apathy to empathy whenever you feel a wave of impatience with others come over you:

1. Imagine a feather in the palm of your hand, your hand close to your mouth.

2. As you open your mouth to speak, as you breathe out, the feather flutters and lifts off your hand on the currents of your breath and words.

3. Now imagine how this happens (symbolically) with people: they are like feathers – sensitive, unnerved by some of your more blunt or straight-down-the-line words, which can hurt or turn them against you. They overreact; like the feather, they get blown away or swirl out of control.

When you begin to recognise the insensitive, outspoken you who disturbs the feather, you'll be kinder to yourself – and to the 'featherlight' people in life, too.

WISH ON A STAR

To improve all love relationships or to ensure a commitment or loyalty, perform this simple ritual on the night of a new crescent moon – the perfect timing for Aries love to develop.

You will need:
* A piece of tiger's eye
* A red candle

1. On the night of a new crescent moon, light the candle, and place the tiger's eye beside it.

2. If you can go outside, take the crystal and candle with you, gaze at the stars and focus on the one that seems to twinkle or shine brightest and best for you. If you stay inside, imagine the constellations above you, and one star that stands out from all the others.

3. Place the candle on a flat surface, then hold the tiger's eye up to the sky as you make your wish for commitment, loyalty or improvement in a relationship, or whatever it is you are truly seeking in love.

4. Repeat the wish a total of three times, and then focus on the candle flame for a few moments to seal your wish to the Universe.

By the full moon, you will discover that someone is as true to you as you are true to them.

....

AROUSE SOME PASSION

To restore or rekindle passion or invite it into your love life, try invoking the sensual power of Eros, the god of erotic love. Here's how:

You will need:
* 8 small, rough ruby or red carnelian crystals
* A red candle

1. On a table or somewhere they won't be disturbed, place the eight crystals in the shape of an arrow pointing towards the west.

2. Place the red candle at the point of the arrow. (So you should have four crystals in a row and two in two angled lines on either side of the point to mark the arrow head.)

3. Light the candle and say: 'I point this arrow where love grows, so Eros bring me joy with your bow'.

4. Focus on the arrow crystals for a few minutes, then pick up the four angled crystals and place them at the other end of the point, now facing east. Move the candle to the point at the east and say: 'I point this arrow to bring passion to me, the power of sensuality for us will be'.

5. Be mindful of your desire for passion for a few minutes, then blow out the candle.

6. Leave the arrow in place overnight and experience sensual bliss. Once you have performed this ritual, passion will ignite your love life, and your fiery, seductive spirit will attract the kind of physical excitement you crave.

PART TWO

Caring For Your Body

'Be patient, for the world
is broad and wide.'

William Shakespeare, *Romeo and Juliet*

H ere, you will discover alternative ways to look after and nurture your body, not just as a physical presence, but its connection to mind and spirit, too. This section gives you a wide range of ideas, from using sun-sign crystals to protect your physical and psychic self to fitness, diet and beauty tips. There are specific chakra practices and yoga poses especially suited to your sun sign, not forgetting bath-time rituals and calming practices to destress you and nurture holistic wellbeing.

It's often said that all Aries needs is to get down to the gym, work out and run fast, but the true tonics you need for good physical health are fresh air and competition. Because of your high energy levels and awareness of body image, your physical self is usually in pretty good shape. But here are some ways to improve your overall physical wellbeing.

Fitness and Movement

If you're not already doing some form of aerobic exercise, then walking, running, cycling, athletics or other competitive sports are a must to tone those muscles and give you plenty of outlets to unleash your fiery spirit. Other great ways to express this feisty energy are through the martial arts (such as tae kwon do or karate), not forgetting competitive cycling, mountaineering, Nordic walking, skiing and other fast-paced sports, especially those where you as an individual can win.

HILL WALKING

There's nothing more restorative for the Aries spirit than a long hike across the countryside. If you set out alone, do let others know where you are going and which route you are taking, for safety's sake. However, as you like to lead others, maybe organise a few friends, and lead your team to some glorious destination.

If you don't live near the countryside, then find a local park, green space or some streets with trees or vegetation to take a brisk walk. The exchange of energy between plants, tree life and your fighter spirit will vitalise and invigorate all your senses.

....

WARRIOR POSE

If you don't already practise yoga, then now's the time to have a go. Maybe use an app to learn all you need to know about it, so you can be one up on your pals! Here's a pose to get you started:

1. Stand tall with feet together, hands by your side.

2. Take a large step forward with your right leg, so your feet are just over a metre apart.

3. Bend your right knee, keeping it over your ankle, keeping the hips facing to the side.

4. Extend your right arm to the front and left arm behind you. Soften your shoulders down your back and gaze forwards. Stay in this pose for a round of three or four breaths to strengthen and stretch inner thighs and hips.

5. Return to standing and repeat on the other side.

The warrior is a pose you can do between longer yoga sessions, and you don't especially need a mat. It will ground you and remind you of your Aries spirit.

MINDFULNESS THROUGH MOVEMENT

Asking an Arian to sit and meditate for more than a few minutes may pose quite a challenge. (Although maybe that kind of challenge will motivate you to do so?)

Here's a form of mindfulness that might suit you better, based on the practice of a Buddhist walking meditation known as 'kinhin'. This is a very, very slow walk, where you focus on the experience of taking each step.

1. Make two fists with your with palms facing down to the ground and hold them close to your navel. Then open your right hand and close it over your left fist, holding your left fist tightly against your belly.

2. Walk forwards very, very slowly – slower than a tortoise – and be conscious of your heels as they touch the ground. Be aware of every sensation from the muscles or movement in your legs. Feel the weight shift from one part of your foot to the other, from one leg to the other, and take the next step as slowly as the first.

3. Continue for another twelve paces, say, and then retrace your steps, continuing as long as you wish.

Even a few minutes of this practice every day is beneficial for body awareness. As you notice the motions in your body, you will inevitably begin to get impatient with this slow-motion walk. You may well find it jolly irritating as it slows down your normal pace. You may be aware not only of your own reactions to the snail's pace, but how out of balance you feel or how uneven the ground is. Just observe these sensations and reactions, but don't react to your reactions; just be mindful of them.

You can use body awareness when you engage in more competitive or fast-paced sports. Just being mindful of your physical sensations, reactions and how the exercise you choose to undertake affects your moods will help to enhance skill and subdue any emotional feedback that can upset your balance.

SWEAT IT OUT

You may find joy in sweating out those negative or unwanted emotions that often boil up inside you, such as resentment or anger. One way to release grudges and feelings of being wronged is to literally jump in the hot tub or sauna or try out some hot yoga. While you're dripping with sweat, focus first on the forgiveness of others, and then forgive yourself for whatever is 'getting to you'. As you unwind in the heat, experiencing a physical release, your emotions will be released, too, and you will begin to replace negativity with a positive light for the future.

Nutrition

Aries thrives on 'little-and-often'-type meals, but make sure you eat quality food to boost your metabolism and vitalise your energetic lifestyle. Mealtimes are not set in stone for you. In fact, with such a busy schedule, it's no wonder you tend to prefer snacks and quick-fix meals, over sitting down to a formal dinner. However, the one meal that you would benefit from taking your time over is breakfast, which will set you up with lasting energy for the day ahead.

AVOCADO TOAST FOR BREAKFAST

As Aries is usually first to try something new, while your pals may be indulging in yoghurt and oat drinks, you can discover the benefits of this simple, healthy start to the day.

Avocados are full of potassium (which helps to lower high blood pressure, often a niggling effect of the Aries non-stop lifestyle). Simply mash the avocado with a little olive oil and a touch of lime juice, prepare your toast, then generously pile the avocado mash on to it. Top with ground cayenne pepper or a sprinkling of Tabasco/ hot chilli sauce and a drizzle of olive oil. A simple, healthy and zippy start to the active Aries day.

OUTDOOR SNACK

As Arians spend as much time as they can outdoors, whether for exhilarating sports or just to enjoy the fresh air, here's a quickly thrown together and nutritious sandwich to pop in your rucksack or sports bag.

You will need:

* Your favourite bread
* Some roast beef slices, smoked salmon or trout
* Or, if you are vegetarian, hard-boiled and mashed eggs
* Or, if you're vegan, some chopped red and green pepper
* Horseradish sauce

When assembling your sandwich, smother your chosen filling with the horseradish sauce to give you vitalising, fiery energy. Horseradish is known to boost circulation and metabolism – just what Arians need to get their physical goals achieved.

CHAKRA BALANCE

The body's chakras are the epicentres of the life-force energy that flows through all things (see p. 20).

The chakra most associated with Aries (and your ruler, Mars) is the solar-plexus chakra. Situated midway between your navel and chest, this chakra is the seat of personal power. It aligns with your spirited energy and sense of 'I do' and 'I will do it now'.

If your solar-plexus chakra is balanced, you'll feel confident and motivated. You will be ready to take on the world or a whole new range of projects (perhaps never quite managing to finish them, but your enthusiasm will be boundless). To maintain chakra harmony, hold a sunstone (representing confidence) to your belly when you focus on your mission.

When the solar-plexus chakra is underactive, you're more like a lost sheep than a potent ram. You lack the energy to get up and go, and everything and everyone gets to you. Niggled by other people's problems or opinions, you worry about failing before you've even begun. To boost the chakra, wear or carry orange topaz for self-empowerment. This will restore your outgoing nature, enhance self-respect, expressive creativity and bless you with a strong sense of personal power.

When this chakra is overactive, you are bossy, irritable, careless, reckless and quick to anger. To subdue it, carry or wear amber (to absorb and disperse negativity). Hold it to your navel, and imagine an amber light flowing through you, from head to toe. Each time you exhale, negativity will be released from your body.

Beauty

They say beauty is in the eye of the beholder, and Aries always has an eye on themselves, whether in the mirror or a vision of how they like to look – and that's stunning.

You're pretty clued up about what suits you and the kind of image you want to express, but here are a few tips to help you recharge your batteries or simply care about being the best of yourself.

....

A GOOD NIGHT'S SLEEP

While you sleep, your epidermis is repairing itself, rebuilding collagen and increasing blood flow to help remove UV exposure and age damage. So even though Aries thrives on little sleep, you would still benefit from a night of peace, calm and pleasant dreams to recharge your batteries and improve your skin.

Try the crystal arrangement below. You will wake up revitalised.

You will need:
* A howlite crystal
* 2 amethyst crystals
* A moonstone crystal

1. Place an amethyst crystal in each of the corners of the room closest to your pillow.

2. Place the other two stones in the remaining two corners of your room.

Howlite repairs stressed skin and prevents insomnia; amethyst brings healing energy to your dreams; and moonstone removes emotional tension, helping you to drift off.

....

RELAXATION RITUAL

With so much energy to expend, it's hardly surprising you don't have much time to relax – why sit back and twiddle your thumbs when, as an Aries, you could be doing something exciting?

However, a relaxing bath-time ritual will restore you physically, nurture your skin and promote an inner sense of beauty, ensuring you're ready for anything on your next mission.

You will need:
* A glass of bubbly, green tea or whatever you enjoy most
* 2 pink candles
* Any bath products you enjoy
* Patchouli essential oil
* Ylang-ylang essential oil
* 2 rose-quartz crystals

1. Prepare or pour your drink.

2. Place one candle at the head of the bath and one at the foot.

3. Light the candles and, as you run your bath, add a few drops of the oils to the water, along with your chosen bath products.

4. Sink into the bath and place the two rose quartz crystals in the water either side of you to balance and promote calming energy throughout your body.

Stay in the bath as long as you like, sipping your drink and delighting in 'me-time' and body restoration.

RED HOT

Looking fabulous and putting on a glamorous show brings the Aries spirit to life. So to enhance your fiery flame, go paint the town red.

Wear red – whether lipstick, hair colour, shoes or outfit – to inspire and invigorate the inner you. Try a splash of glitter or an iridescent red shimmer in your make-up palette or treat your hair to a vibrant new shade of red, and you'll be sure to win any head-turning competition. And carry or wear red carnelian or ruby jewellery to amplify all aspects of your colourful character.

General Wellbeing

The Ram tends to focus on physical fitness and appearance, forgetting that their environment can have an impact on their energy levels, too.

But this works both ways, as your personal dynamic energy flow has an influence on your local surroundings too.

So to maintain a healthy connection and balance between the inner you and the outer environment, the following practices will ensure your general wellbeing is cared for.

DECLUTTER

The Ram at home or at work can create quite a mess – heaps of clothes on the floor or chair, books and papers strewn across tables and so on. (They also rather like the idea of someone else clearing up after them.) But the more mess there is around them, the less room they'll have to stretch, relax or strut about in.

Decluttering is a matter of choice, and it can be fun deciding what you need now, what you won't need until the future and what you don't need at all. So write a list (you know how you love a list), then get to work – and be ruthless (you're good at that, too!):

1. Cross things off the list as you chuck them out.

2. Cross things off the list as you store them away.

3. Cross things off that don't need to be on the list.

4. Next, move furniture around, clear spaces and try to create areas where you can walk about freely.

5. Once you are satisfied, chuck the list away – that in itself will give you an awe-inspiring sense of freedom.

6. Perform a smudging session (see Glossary, p. 119) to cleanse the home of any negative energy: walk around your home or workspace with a sage smudging stick (see Resources, p. 117) and wave it gently in all corners to purify and cleanse.

Like any spring clean (remember, Aries represents springtime and the clearing away of winter), a good declutter will give you the initiative to think about new goals and boost your energy levels into the bargain.

EMPOWERMENT RITUAL

Even Aries can feel exhausted and need some time off from their madcap racing around. So once you've given yourself a break (yes, you are allowed to relax for a day or just flop on the sofa – the only person stopping you is you), revitalise your physical energy levels with this restorative crystal ritual.

You will need:
* 3 pieces of bloodstone
* 3 pieces of tiger's eye
* 3 pieces of sunstone
* 3 pieces of clear quartz crystal
* A pouch

1. Take your crystals to a sunny spot outside, and place them in a circle around you, alternating bloodstone, tiger's eye, sunstone, clear quartz and so on.

2. Standing in the middle of the circle, turn first to the north and say, 'Energies of the north empower me with strength'.

3. Next, turn to the east and say, 'Energies of the east empower me with spirit'.

4. Next, turn to the south and say, 'Energies of the south empower me with stamina'.

5. Turn to the west and say, 'Energies of the west empower me with brilliance'.

6. Return to face north and pick up the crystals one by one in a clockwise direction. Keep them safely in your pouch for the next time you need a burst of vitality from the Universe.

Once you have completed this ritual you will feel empowered – ready for action and fired up with enthusiasm and passion for your next goal.

SELF-LOVE POTION

Choosing to do something rather than nothing ensures you are focused, energised and alert. You like to look good and keep yourself in shape, but sometimes your fast-track lifestyle means you don't have time to look after your sensual side, which can get ignored, repressed or totally forgotten in the race for success.

In times of stress or frantic activity, dab this magic potion on your wrists or behind your knees to polish all your senses, as you would your golden trophies.

You will need:
* A small phial or lidded bottle
* Almond oil
* Myrtle essential oil
* Rose essential oil
* A piece of amber

1. Fill the little bottle nearly to the top with almond oil (this is your base oil).

2. Add a few drops each of the myrtle and rose oils, then put the lid on the phial and shake vigorously. Leave overnight.

3. The next day, dab a few drops of oil on to the amber. When it has dried, place the amber in your pocket or bag.

4. Throughout your busy day, hold the amber tightly in your hand to vitalise your senses.

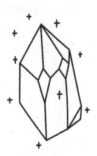

PART THREE

Caring For Your Soul

The real voyage of discovery consists
not in seeking new landscapes,
but in having new eyes.

Marcel Proust, French novelist

This final section offers you tailored, fun, easy and amazing ways to connect to and care for your sacred self. This, in turn, means you will begin to feel at one with the joyous energy of the Universe. You don't have to sign up to any religion or belief system (unless you want to) – just take some time to experience uplifting moments through your interaction with the spiritual aspects of the cosmos. Care for your sun sign's soul centre, and you care about the Universe, too.

Like the other Fire signs, Sagittarius and Leo, the Ram's solar purpose is driven by an inner flame, burning bright optimism for the future. Arians are instinctively aware of this flame within, which is expressed through their fiery self-confidence and their quest for making personal dreams come true.

As you're often the first to discover new spiritual trends, it may be that you already have an eclectic collection of belief systems. And why not? At the end of the day, they all lead to an understanding of our connection to the Universe, whether you call it divine, a named deity, animism, ch'i, zen or an encounter with danger.

Caring for this intangible awareness of what your sacred self or soul is all about isn't simple. After all, you can't take it for a bike ride or pin it down to a place and time. So maybe you just have to experience 'it' on that bike ride, be aware of 'it' as you rush off on another adventure and realise that 'it' is there within you.

Here are some rituals and practices to bring you closer to that soul sensation.

....

ENHANCING INTUITION

Being blessed with intuition, you often find yourself in the right place at the right time. Following a hunch is always a gamble, but then you wouldn't be a true Aries if you didn't take risks. And usually, those hunches are right for the purpose intended at the time – so let's look at ways in which you can boost your intuitive side.

* **Don't stifle a hunch.** When you get an intuitive hunch, your head may challenge that flash of insight rather than trusting in it. Before that happens, ask yourself: what did that feeling bring up for you? What did the hunch mean? If you felt an instant sense of positivity, then follow the moment. It's right.
* **Stay true to your values.** Sometimes the Aries impulsiveness has very little to do with your values and can lead you astray. Imagine you go out on a date, for example; on impulse, you agree to meet up again, but when you get home, you realise this person isn't for you, and that the value you place on love, desire, mutual attraction and so on has been overpowered by mere whimsy. In that situation in future, before you speak, recall the word 'value' – just for a moment or

two – because it comes from the same source as intuition, deep within.

* **Read people.** Before you get to know someone, or even if you're just in a crowd and see someone across the room, what are your feelings about them? What energy are they giving off? Can you sense their aura, or their power? What about them is either attractive or doesn't resonate with you? The more you practise 'reading' people and situations, the more you'll realise how much you already know through your intuition.

Intuition is one of the best connections to your deepest sacred self; it will enable you to experience those moments of being at one with the Universe.

SPIRIT FRIEND

In many spiritual traditions, specific animals are considered sacred and their spirits believed to protect and guide the individual or clan. Aries is renowned for travelling or acting alone; but admit it – maybe you need some spiritual guidance or help from the Universe at times? Whether you believe in guardian spirit animals or not, this simple practice invites you to embrace the possibility of having a guide you can 'conjure up' or call on for support or help with making positive decisions. This spirit friend may appear as your cat, the butterfly that lands on a flower, the bee that buzzes outside your window – but whatever form it takes, whether imaginary, real or supernatural, an opening up and acceptance of this kind of awareness will enable you to listen to the messages the Universe is sending you.

You will need:

* An image of your spirit guide (spirit animals associated with Aries are: tiger, hawk, wolf and ram; choose one of these or any other that you think will inspire and protect you)
* A small clear quartz crystal

1. To befriend your spirit guide, place the image on a table.

2. For a few moments, focus on the image and send out positive feelings.

3. Take up the crystal, place it on the image and say: 'My spirit friend will protect me in all moments when I need their guidance'.

4. Gaze into the crystal, visualise your spirit animal living within the crystal, always there to guard and advise you.

5. Take up the crystal, now imbued with the energy of your animal, and say: 'Thank you spirit guide for coming into my life'.

Take the crystal with you wherever you go, or when you need to make any choice that requires friendly advice. When you hold the crystal in your hand for a few moments, the spirit will tell you the answer.

....

TREE TALK

Trees come in all shapes and sizes. If you're lucky enough to live near woods and trees, then you're off to a good start for engaging in the universal energy that flows through Nature, by talking to and literally touching, caressing or hugging a tree.

Aries is curious about any new adventure, so set off whenever the urge takes you and find a tree that 'speaks' to you. It may be a giant oak, a young sycamore or a straggly willow – whatever species it is, if you feel an affinity with it, then be at one with it: touch its bark, its leaves, hug its trunk, speak words of love to it. Show you care about it, as much as you care about yourself. Thank the tree for being there, and for its grounding energy.

Under your tree, say, 'I am grateful for the Earth and the sacredness of all. I am a part of this Universe, like the tree.'

After your communication with the tree, you will begin to experience an affinity with many other plants, wildlife or even whole landscapes, and realise your spiritual connection with Nature.

LUNAR AND SOLAR RITUAL

Even brash Fire signs need time to connect to the receptive, gentler energies of the moon. By embracing this mystical, magical lunar power, you will feel more at home with your soul.

This ritual reminds you how the two heavenly bodies, sun and moon, are woven into our perception of the world. The sun is associated with light, the moon with the dark; and similarly in astrology – the sun with how we shine and the moon with how we feel.

To enrich your spirit and soul, perform this ritual during a full-moon phase if possible.

You will need:
* A bowl of water
* A white candle
* A moonstone
* A sunstone

1. On the evening of the full moon, place your bowl of water (representing the moon) in an outside space.

2. Light the candle (representing the sun).

3. Place the moonstone in the water first, then the sunstone, and say: 'I am connected to spirit and soul, to sun and to moon and to my sacred self'.

4. For a few moments, contemplate the full moon, and how the light of the sun illuminates it. (If you can't see the full moon, imagine it instead.) Imagine the sun and the moon are deep within you, always dancing in rhythm, always bringing you into their cycle of new to full moon, full to new moon, and showing you the way to the soul and spirit of yourself.

5. Take the two stones out of the water and blow out the candle.

Keep the stones in a prominent place where you can see them every day. They will energise and endow you with a sense of spirit (the sunstone, the fiery spirit of Aries) and soul (the moonstone, the gentle Ram that hides within you). Caring for both the spirit and soul of yourself means you will feel a deeper connection to both aspects of Aries within you.

RED CORAL VISUALISATION

One of the most beautiful gifts in the sea is the vibrant red or precious coral, under threat from harvesting, intensive fishing and climate change. For Aries, coral symbolises the hidden side of you – the receptive, intuitive fire that burns within and which needs protecting, too. Accept and nurture this inner fire, and you will discover the profound happiness of being yourself.

Simply visualise red coral bushes on a dark, rocky seabed or deep within underwater caverns, its fiery colour bringing life to the shadowy world. Visualise the coral as the red fire that glows within you, surrounded by the ocean of all life. In this image, you are at one with the world and all that's in it.

Last Words

The Aries self-care journey is one that has to be as straightforward as any adventure you choose to go on. This book has taken you down a simple route, where self-acceptance, navigating your feelings and being more compromising will enable you to see that 'self-care' isn't just about fitness and body image (although it is that, too), but about understanding who you as an Aries. This little guide has also shown you ways to care about the spiritual fire within you, an ability to both nurture and enjoy the experience of something intangible and mysterious, and which will bring you 'alive' in other ways besides the physical.

You have learned how to enjoy, indulge in and care for the extrovert qualities of your sign, allowing you to embrace your formidable spirit and inspirational soul, while accepting your limitations, so that you can forge your way ahead to a brilliant future.

Take every experience in life as one to shape, define and enhance the archetypal Aries you are becoming.

It's exciting to discover one's true potential and say, 'Hey, it's ok to be me' – free of the constraints of other people's expectations. It's awe-inspiring to know that you can be the outrageous, fun-loving and aspirational person you are. And by accepting who you are and trying out the best ways to inspirit that Aries character, you are actually on the road to looking after 'number one' in the best possible way, too.

For you, Aries, self-care is a journey of self-realisation, so enjoy the adventure you are on – that, in itself, shows you truly care.

Resources

Main sites for crystals, stones, candles, smudging sticks, incense, pouches, essential oils and everything needed for the holistic self-care practices included in this book:
holisticshop.co.uk
thepsychictree.co.uk
thesoulangels.co.uk
earthcrystals.com
livrocks.com
artisanaromatics.com

For a substantial range of books (and metaphysical items) on astrology, divination, runes, palmistry, tarot and holistic health, etc.:
thelondonastrologyshop.com
watkinsbooks.com
mysteries.co.uk
barnesandnoble.com
innertraditions.com

For more information on astrology, personal horo-
scopes and birth-chart calculations:
astro-charts.com (simplest, very user friendly)

horoscopes.astro-seek.com
(straightforward)
astrolibrary.org/free-birth-chart
(easy to use, with lots of extra information)

Glossary

Aura An invisible electromagnetic energy field that emanates from and surrounds all living beings

Auric power The dominant colour of the aura, which reveals your current mood or state

Chakra Sanskrit for 'wheel', in Eastern spiritual traditions the seven chakras are the main epicentres – or wheels – of invisible energy throughout the body

Dark of the moon This is when the moon is invisible to us, due to its proximity to the sun; it is a time for reflection, solitude and a deeper awareness of oneself

Divination Gaining insight into the past, present and future using symbolic or esoteric means

Double-terminator crystal A quartz crystal with a point at each end, allowing its energy to flow both ways

Full moon The sun is at its maximum opposition to the moon, thus casting light across all of the moon's orb; in esoteric terms, it is a time for culmination, finalising deals, committing to love and so on

Geopathic stress Negative energy emanating from and on the Earth, such as underground water courses, tunnels, overhead electrical cables and geological faults

Grid A specific pattern or layout of items symbolising specific intentions or desires

Horoscope An astrological chart or diagram showing the position of the sun, moon and planets at the time of any given event, such as the moment of somebody's birth, a marriage or the creation of an enterprise; it is used to interpret the characteristics or to forecast the future of that person or event

New crescent moon A fine sliver of crescent light that appears curving outwards to the right in the northern hemisphere and to the left in the southern hemisphere; this phase is for beginning new projects, new romance, ideas and so on

Psychic energy One's intuition, sixth sense or instincts, as well as the divine, numinous or magical power that flows through everything

Shadow side In astrology, your shadow side describes those aspects of your personality associated with your opposite sign and of which you are not usually aware

Smudging Clearing negative energy from the home with a smouldering bunch of dried herbs, such as sage

Solar return salutation A way to give thanks and welcome the sun's return to your zodiac sign once a year (your birthday month)

Sun in opposition The sun as it moves through the opposite sign to your own sun sign

Sun sign The zodiac sign through which the sun was moving at the exact moment of your birth

Waning moon The phase of the moon after it is full, when it begins to lose its luminosity – the waning moon is illuminated on its left side in the northern hemisphere, and on its right side in the southern hemisphere; this is a time for letting go, acceptance and preparing to start again

Waxing moon The phase between a new and a full moon, when it grows in luminosity – the waxing moon is illuminated on its right side in the northern hemisphere and on its left side in the southern hemisphere; this is a time for putting ideas and desires into practice

Zodiac The band of sky divided into twelve segments (known as the astrological signs), along which the paths of the sun, the moon and the planets appear to move

About the Author

After studying at the Faculty of Astrological Studies in London, the UK, Sarah gained the Diploma in Psychological Astrology – an in-depth 3-year professional training programme cross-fertilised by the fields of astrology and depth, humanistic and transpersonal psychology. She has worked extensively in the media as astrologer for titles such as *Cosmopolitan* magazine (UK), *SHE, Spirit & Destiny* and the *London Evening Standard*, and appeared on UK TV and radio shows, including *Steve Wright in the Afternoon* on BBC Radio 2.

Her mainstream mind-body-spirit books include the international bestsellers, *The Tarot Bible, The Little Book of Practical Magic* and *Secrets of the Universe in 100 Symbols*.

Sarah currently practises and teaches astrology and other esoteric arts in the heart of the countryside.

Acknowledgements

I would first like to thank everyone at Yellow Kite, Hodder & Stoughton and Hachette UK who were part of the process of creating this series of twelve zodiac self-care books. I am especially grateful to Carolyn Thorne for the opportunity to write these guides; Anne Newman for her editorial advice, which kept me 'carefully' on the right track; and Olivia Nightingall who kept me on target for everything else! It is when people come together with their different skills and talents that the best books are made – so I am truly grateful for being part of this team.

See the full Astrology Self-Care series here

9781399704885   9781399704915   9781399704588

9781399704618   9781399704649   9781399704670

9781399704700   9781399704731   9781399704762

9781399704793   9781399704823   9781399704854

books to help you live a good life

Join the conversation and tell
us how you live a #goodlife

🐦 @yellowkitebooks
📘 YellowKiteBooks
📌 Yellow Kite Books
📷 YellowKiteBooks